FIND OUT ABOUT

ANCIENT

ROME

JANE BINGHAM

HODDER
Wayland

an imprint of Hodder Children's Books

First published in 2006 by Hodder Wayland,
an imprint of Hodder Children's Books

© Hodder Wayland 2006

Project Editor: Kirsty Hamilton
Designer: Simon Borrough
Maps: Peter Bull

British Library Cataloguing in Publication Data
Bingham, Jane
Find out about ancient Rome
1.Rome – Civilization – Juvenile literature 2.Rome –
History – Juvenile literature 3.Rome – Antiques –
Juvenile literature
I.Title II.Ancient Rome
937

ISBN 07502 47568

Colour Reproduction by Dot Gradations Ltd, UK
Printed in China

Hodder Children's Books
A division of Hodder Headline Limited
338 Euston Road, London NW1 3BH

The publisher would like to thank the following for permission to reproduce their pictures: Title page, 9, Jonathan Blair / Corbis; 4, ML Sinbaldi / Corbis; 6, Adam Woolfitt / Corbis; 7, Jeffrey L. Rotman / Corbis; 8, akg-images; 10, 43, Bettmann / Corbis; 11, 22, 26, 27, 31, 37, Araldo de Luca / Corbis; 12,14, 41, Charles and Josette Lenars / Corbis; 13, Vittoriano Rastelli / Corbis; 15, Homer Sykes / Corbis; 16, Seamus Culligan / ZUMA / Corbis; 17, 32, 38, 39, Mimmo Jodice / Corbis; 18, James L. Amos / Corbis; 19, Dave Bartruff / Corbis; 20, 25, Roger Wood / Corbis; 21, 34, Macduff Everton / Corbis; 23, 33, akg-images / Erich Lessing; 24, Eriol Ciol / Corbis; 28, Archivo Iconografico, S.A. / Corbis; 29, akg-images / Robert O'Dea; 30, Richard Hamilton Smith / Corbis; 35, Sandro Vannini / Corbis; 36, Gustavo Tomsich / Corbis; 40, CRDPHOTO / Corbis; 42, Christie's Images / Corbis; 44, 45, John & Dallas Heaton / Corbis;

CONTENTS

WHO WERE
THE ROMANS?
4-7

HOW WERE
THE ROMANS
RULED?
8-11

HOW DID
THE ROMANS
EXTEND THEIR RULE?
12-15

WHAT WAS LIFE LIKE
FOR THE ROMANS?
16-31

HOW DID
THE ROMANS
COMMUNICATE?
32-35

WHO DID
THE ROMANS
WORSHIP?
36-41

WHAT DID
THE ROMANS
CONTRIBUTE
TO THE WORLD?
42-45

TIMELINE
FIND OUT MORE
46

GLOSSARY
47

INDEX
48

WHO WERE THE ROMANS?

The first Romans were farmers and hunters who belonged to a tribe called the Latins. Around 750BC, the Latins began to settle on the banks of the River Tiber, in the land that is now Italy.

Gradually, this settlement grew into the city of Rome and the Latins became known as 'Romans'.

ETRUSCANS AND GREEKS

The Romans were strongly influenced by two older civilizations: the Etruscans and the ancient Greeks. The Etruscans lived in northern Italy and were great traders, architects and engineers. They passed on their knowledge of these subjects to the Romans, who also copied the Etruscan customs of holding chariot races and gladiator fights.

The land to the south of Rome was dominated by the Greeks who had set up

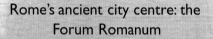

Rome's ancient city centre: the Forum Romanum

WHAT DOES IT TELL US?

The Forum Romanum (shown here) was the grandest of all the public squares in Rome. Its oldest buildings date from around 500BC and by the time of the Roman Empire it was filled with impressive government buildings, temples, and shops. Even though these structures are now in ruins, they still give an idea of the power and glory of ancient Rome.

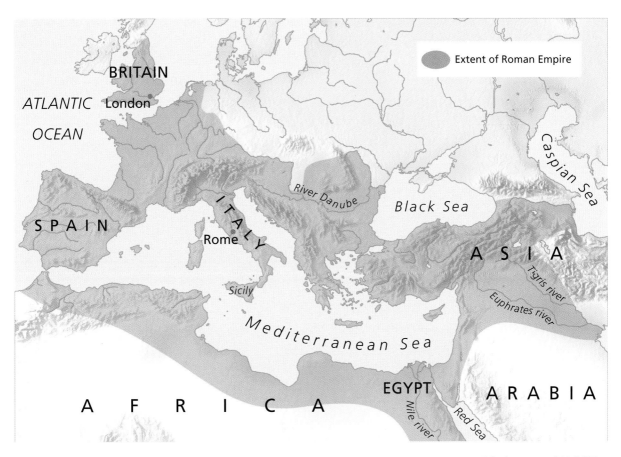

A This map shows the Roman Empire at its largest, under the emperor Hadrian in AD117.

colonies there. The Greeks had established a magnificent civilization based around the city of Athens, which flourished from the eighth to the third century BC. However, by 140BC Greece had become part of the Roman world. Roman art, architecture and religion were all strongly influenced by the ancient Greeks, while Roman thinkers and scientists copied many ideas from the Greeks.

THE RISE OF THE ROMANS

By the third century BC, Rome was a wealthy city, but it was surrounded by enemy tribes. Gradually, the Romans conquered all their enemies and gained control of Italy. Then they fought wars to win land in northern Africa and what is now called Spain. By the year 31BC, when Augustus became first Emperor of Rome, the Romans controlled most of the area around the Mediterranean Sea. Over the next 150 years the Romans created a vast and powerful empire.

The Roman Empire reached its largest size in AD117, under the emperor Hadrian. At that time, the Empire stretched from Britain in the north to northern Africa in the south, and reached as far east as present-day Iraq.

ROMAN CITIES

Wherever the Romans conquered, they set up towns and cities that were modeled on Rome, and introduced the Roman way of life. Each area (or province) of the Empire was ruled by a governor, while members of the Roman army kept the peace. The governors made sure that all the people in their provinces paid their taxes, obeyed the Roman laws, and respected the Roman gods.

All over the Empire the Romans built well-planned cities and towns. Each town had its own public buildings and temples, as well as houses, shops and snack bars. Most towns had a set of public baths, while the larger cities had a theatre and an arena (for shows and races). Roman towns had fresh running water in their fountains and baths, and a system of underground sewers.

A provincial city: ruins of Arausio

WHAT DO THEY TELL US?

A triumphal arch and a theatre survive from the Roman city of Arausio, (now the city of Orange, in southern France). The remains of these grand buildings (as seen below) show that the Romans built great cities in the provinces, and didn't just concentrate all their efforts on Rome.

WHAT DO THEY TELL US?

This deep-sea diver is holding a ceramic jar, known as an amphora. Jars like this were used by Roman merchants to store grain and oil.

TRADE AND TRADERS

Trade was very important in the Roman Empire, and goods of all kinds were brought into Rome. The most important trading goods were grain, olive oil and wine, but there were also more exotic items, such as spices from the East, silk from China, and ivory from Africa. Every part of the Empire was linked to Rome by road, river or sea, and some adventurous Roman merchants reached as far as Scandinavia and Russia.

DECLINE AND FALL

By the fourth century AD the Roman Empire was weakening. Meanwhile, warlike tribes from the north were launching savage attacks on the Roman provinces. In 395 the Empire split permanently into two. The western half was ruled from Rome and the eastern half had its capital in Constantinople (present-day Istanbul). The western Empire came to an end in 476, when the city of Rome was invaded by a tribe of Visigoths. The Empire in the east lasted for another thousand years. However, as the memory of the Roman Empire faded, it became known as the Byzantine Empire.

HOW WERE THE ROMANS RULED ?

Early Rome was ruled by kings. The king was chosen by a group of elders who also formed a council to advise the king. No accurate records exist for this period, but, according to Roman legend there were seven kings of Rome and the last three were Etruscans.

Under the Etruscan kings, Rome became a powerful, well-run city. However, the Roman people hated being ruled by the Etruscans, and the last king was the most unpopular of all. Known as Tarquinus Superbus (Tarquin the Proud), he ruled without consulting the council and put to death anyone he pleased. Eventually the Roman people decided to drive Tarquin out of the city around the year 510BC. They swore they would never be ruled by a king again.

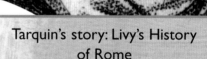

Tarquin's story: Livy's History of Rome

WHAT DOES IT TELL US?

We know the story of Tarquin through the writings of Livy. He was a historian (shown here), who lived five hundred years after Tarquin ruled. Livy's massive *History of Rome* was partly based on folktales handed down by generations of Romans. His account is full of dramatic scenes, such as Tarquin hurling the previous king down the council steps to his death.

WHAT DOES IT TELL US?

The initials SPQR were carved on buildings and statues during the Roman Republic, and the same letters can still be seen in the streets of Rome today. SPQR stands for 'Senatus Populusque Romanus', which is Latin for 'The senate and the people of Rome'. These initials reminded people that the city belonged not only to the Senate but also to the ordinary Roman people.

⋎ During the Republic, Rome was ruled by a group of powerful senators who were elected by the Roman people. This sculpture shows the head of a Roman senator.

THE ROMAN REPUBLIC

After the Roman people had banished Tarquin, they set up the Roman Republic, which lasted for over four hundred years. The Republic was ruled by the senate, a group of powerful men (called senators) who came from Rome's most important families. Within the senate, two leaders – known as consuls – were chosen to rule Rome each year.

Most Romans believed that it was much better to be ruled by a senate than by a king. But not everyone was happy. The ordinary Roman people – known as the plebeians – wanted more power. Some plebeians led riots against the senate and even threatened to set up a city of their own. In 366BC a Plebeian Council was established to represent the views of the ordinary people. After 287BC all decisions of the Plebeian Council had to become law – even if the senate didn't agree.

THE END OF THE REPUBLIC

By the second century BC, the Roman Republic was facing problems. The Roman lands were growing fast and becoming hard to control. Meanwhile, powerful army generals were hungry for more power – and the most ambitious of all was Julius Caesar.

In 49BC, Julius Caesar marched with his army to Rome and seized power. He made good laws to help the poor, but in 44BC he declared himself ruler for life. A group of Roman senators feared that Caesar was becoming much too powerful, so they hatched a plot to kill him.

▲ Julius Caesar was an excellent general and leader of men. He is shown here leading the Roman army.

The Death of Caesar: Plutarch's account

WHAT DOES IT TELL US?

Julius Caesar had a very dramatic death. He was stabbed to death in the senate house by the men who used to be his friends. We know the details of his death because of a lively account by the historian, Plutarch (AD46 – 126). In the sixteenth century, William Shakespeare adapted Plutarch's *Life of Caesar* and turned it into a famous play, *Julius Caesar*. Plutarch wrote:

…those who had prepared themselves for the murder bared each of them his dagger, and Caesar, hemmed in on all sides, whichever way he turned confronting blows of weapons aimed at his face and eyes, driven hither and thither like a wild beast, was entangled in the hands of all; for all had to take part in the sacrifice and taste of the slaughter. And the pedestal was drenched with his blood, so that one might have thought that Pompey himself was presiding over this vengeance upon his enemy, who now lay prostrate at his feet, quivering from a multitude of wounds. For it is said that he received twenty-three; and many of the conspirators were wounded by one another, as they struggled to plant all those blows in one body.

GREAT EMPERORS

Following Caesar's death there was a period of conflict, but in 27BC, the Roman Republic came to an end and Augustus was made the first Emperor of Rome. Augustus was a strong and efficient ruler and a great army general. After the death of Augustus, over a hundred emperors ruled from AD14 to AD476.

Some of the Roman emperors were outstanding leaders. In the first century AD, Titus and Trajan led the Roman army in great conquests. Marcus Aurelius, who ruled in the second century AD, was a talented commander and a philosopher, while, in the fourth century, the Emperor Constantine reunited a divided empire and allowed Christians to worship freely.

MAD, BAD AND DANGEROUS

Sadly, not all the Roman Emperors were great men. Tiberius, who became emperor after Augustus, had all his enemies put to death, while the next emperor, Caligula, may have been insane. Nero, who ruled from AD54 to 68, had his wife and mother murdered. In the second century AD, the Emperor Commodus wasted vast amounts of public money on gory gladiator fights and races.

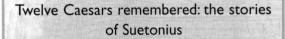

Twelve Caesars remembered: the stories of Suetonius

WHAT DO THEY TELL US?

The Roman historian Suetonius (AD69-140) produced a series of lively portraits of the first twelve Roman emperors, in which he describes their achievements and their weaknesses. In his biography of Caligula, Suetonius depicts the emperor as a crazed monster who once ordered his soldiers to attack the sea. Suetonius' *Lives* were often amusing, but they also had a serious purpose. They revealed that great power could sometimes fall into very dangerous hands.

➤ This statue shows the Emperor Augustus in military dress. By the time of his death in AD41 most people had accepted the idea of being ruled by an emperor.

HOW DID THE ROMANS EXTEND THEIR RULE?

The Romans used their highly efficient army to win lands far away from Rome. Once they had conquered an area, soldiers built strong forts to defend their position. The army also built excellent roads, to connect their newly won lands to the rest of the Roman Empire.

CENTURIES, COHORTS AND LEGIONS

By the time of the Empire, the Roman army was extremely well-organized and its soldiers fought in highly disciplined groups. The smallest unit was the *contuberium* – a group of eight soldiers who all lived and fought together. Ten *contuberia* made up a century (80 men) and six centuries made a cohort (480 men). The largest unit was the legion, which was made up of ten cohorts.

Altogether, the Roman army had a total of 25 to 35 legions, but this number varied at different times of the Empire. As well as soldiers, each legion also included messengers, builders, engineers and doctors.

◁ Roman legionnaires wore metal helmets and breastplates to protect their heads and upper bodies (like the ones in this modern Roman battle re-enactment). On their feet, they had leather sandals studded with nails to give them a better grip.

WHAT DOES IT TELL US?

Julius Caesar (100-44BC) was a great military leader who led campaigns in Spain and Gaul (present-day France) and even reached as far as Britain. He wrote detailed accounts of his military campaigns in seven volumes, called *The Gallic Wars*. Caesar's accounts provide valuable information on how his men were organized.

TYPES OF SOLDIERS

The Roman Imperial army contained several types of soldiers. Foot soldiers, known as legionnaires, fought with swords and javelins (long spears). They wore metal helmets and breastplates and carried large wooden shields to defend themselves. Cavalry soldiers used the same weapons but fought on horseback.

Centurions were in charge of a century (80 men) and led their men into battle, wearing a distinctive helmet with a scarlet horsehair plume. Legates commanded the legions, while generals took charge of a whole army. Legates and generals wore splendid golden helmets, crowned with special crests.

In addition to the fighting men, there were also standard bearers, who carried their legion's emblem, and horn-blowers, who sent signals to the soldiers in battle. These important figures often wore the skin of a lion or a bear.

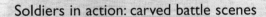

Soldiers in action: carved battle scenes

WHAT DO THEY TELL US?

After winning a battle, the Romans often built a victory column or a triumphal arch to remind people of their great victory. These grand structures were covered with carvings showing scenes from the battle. One of the most famous victory monuments is Trajan's Column in Rome (shown here). It was built around 100AD by the emperor Trajan to celebrate and record his victory over Dacia (in Eastern Europe).

ARMS AND ARMOUR

The Romans didn't just fight with swords and spears. They also had an impressive range of equipment to help them attack an enemy city. Soldiers used massive wooden catapults to hurl heavy stones at their enemies, and smashed down gates and walls with battering rams on wheels. Roman carpenters also built tall wooden siege towers that could be rolled up close to a city's walls. Soldiers inside a siege tower could launch an attack from very close quarters and even climb over the walls to enter an enemy city.

THE TORTOISE FORMATION

Roman army commanders were famous for their brilliant battle tactics, and they used some clever tricks to overcome their

Attack by tortoise: Caesar's account

WHAT DOES IT TELL US?

There are several accounts of the *testudo* (or tortoise formation) being used in battle. The most famous of these comes in Julius Caesar's description of the Roman invasion of Britain in 55BC. Caesar records that his soldiers formed a *testudo* in order to approach the walls of a British fort. This clever tactic clearly paid off because Caesar states that within a few hours the Roman legionnaires had managed to capture the fort. The picture above shows a re-enactment of the famous Roman tortoise formation.

enemies. Sometimes, a group of soldiers would advance in a formation called a *testudo* – or tortoise. The soldiers locked their shields together to form a solid barrier over their heads and around the front of the group. This protected them from enemy spears and allowed the soldiers to get very close to an enemy while remaining unharmed.

BUILDING DEFENCES

Once the Roman army had conquered an area, they had to make sure that their lands remained safe from enemy attacks. They built high walls marking the edge of their territory, and posted soldiers in forts along the walls to defend the Roman lands. One of the most famous Roman defences was Hadrian's Wall, which ran across the north of Britain, marking the northernmost edge of the Empire. It was built by the Emperor Hadrian in the second century AD, in order to keep the warlike northern tribes out of Roman Britain.

Keeping out the enemy: Hadrian's Wall

WHAT DOES IT TELL US?

Hadrian's Wall (shown below) runs for 185 km (115 miles) across the north of England, south of the present-day border with Scotland. For much of its length, the wall has a walkway along the top, where Roman soldiers would have patrolled night and day. There is also a series of forts, built at intervals along the wall, where army units were posted. The wall provides dramatic evidence of the very difficult task that faced the Romans as they tried to keep their Empire safe.

WHAT WAS LIFE LIKE FOR THE ROMANS?

For some fortunate Romans, life was very comfortable. They lived in beautiful town houses or country villas, held lavish banquets, and enjoyed a wide range of leisure activities. However, not everyone lived like this. Most of the people who lived in the Empire had to work very hard to survive.

TOWN LIFE

Roman towns and cities were constructed around grand central squares, which contained impressive public buildings and temples. Stretching out from these squares was a network of streets. Some streets were wide, and flanked by imposing houses that belonged to wealthy citizens. Other streets were much narrower, and lined with shops, workshops and snack bars.

Λ The ruins of a street in Pompeii, southern Italy, showing the remains of shops and workshops.

The poorer people of the town lived above a shop or a workshop, or had rooms in a crowded apartment block. The houses of the rich were built on two levels or more. They had painted walls and mosaic floors and were furnished with couches and low tables. Downstairs, the rooms were arranged around a central courtyard, and included a dining room, a kitchen and sometimes, a bathroom. Upstairs, there were bedrooms for the family. Some town houses also had a garden, where people could relax and meet their friends.

Poorer people lived in small, bare rooms with very little furniture. Unlike the rich, they had no running water or toilets, and no places to cook. Roman apartment blocks were not well built and they often collapsed or caught on fire.

SHOPS AND STALLS

Bakers, butchers, fishmongers, and wine merchants all provided for the citizens' daily needs, and there were also busy markets, where people could buy milk, cheese and vegetables brought into the town by local farmers. Stalls selling snacks were also very popular as most people in towns didn't have a kitchen where they could cook food.

➤ A collection of cooking pots found in Pompeii.

A buried town: Pompeii

WHAT DOES IT TELL US?

In AD79 the Roman city of Pompeii, in southern Italy, was destroyed by a sudden volcanic eruption. The town was showered by burning ash from Mount Vesuvius and most of its citizens were killed instantly. Hundreds of years later, archaeologists began to uncover the ruined town and discovered houses, apartments, shops and workshops all buried under the ash. They also discovered furniture, tools, jewellery and toys that had survived almost intact. Today, most of the town has been excavated and its treasures have been placed in museums. The remains at Pompeii provide a remarkably complete picture of life in a Roman town.

WHAT DOES IT TELL US?

Some exquisite glassware has been found in Roman graves. These objects include delicate flasks and bowls made from multi-coloured glass and inlaid with precious metals. These precious objects show how skilful the Roman glassmakers were. They also illustrate some Romans' belief in the afterlife. When they were buried, rich Romans were equipped with everything they needed for a comfortable existence beyond the grave.

CRAFT WORKERS

In towns all over the Empire, craft workers laboured in workshops to produce a huge variety of goods. Apart from the basic essentials, such as clothes and sandals, pots, pans, and tools, there were also luxury goods. Goldsmiths and silversmiths made elaborate jewellery, glass blowers produced exquisite bowls and goblets, and engravers carved delicate cameo portraits for brooches and rings.

ROMAN BATHS

Very few Roman houses had bathrooms, so people from a variety of social classes in towns paid a daily visit to the public

ʌ The remains of the Roman baths at Bath in southern England.

baths. However, Roman baths were not simply a place to have a good wash. Many of them were very grand buildings with their own gardens, shops and even libraries. People went to the baths to exercise, relax and meet their friends.

A visit to the baths usually began with some vigorous exercise, followed by some time in the *calidarium* – a very hot pool. Instead of using soap, the Romans covered their bodies with oil. Then they used a tool, called a *strigil*, to scrape off all the dirt and the oil. Wealthy Romans brought their slaves to the baths so that the slaves could do the scraping for them.

As well as the *calidarium*, there was also a steam room and a massage area, where people lay on tables and were massaged with oil. Before they left the baths, bathers gradually cooled down in the *tepidarium*, a lukewarm pool, before taking a refreshing dip in the *frigidarium* – an unheated, open-air pool. After they had finished, people might buy a snack at a food stall, read in the library, or relax in the gardens.

Ancient leisure centre: Caracalla's baths

WHAT DO THEY TELL US?

Several examples of Roman baths have survived in cities and towns around the Empire. However, the most impressive baths of all were built in Rome around AD216 by the Emperor Caracalla. This vast leisure complex had room for up to 1,600 people and included art galleries, gymnasiums, gardens, libraries, meeting rooms, and shops. It was decorated throughout with statues and mosaics. Caracalla's baths are now in ruins, but tourists may still gain an impression of their massive size.

COUNTRY LIFE

During the time of the Republic, many Roman families owned small farms in the Italian countryside. Families survived by growing grain and olives and keeping a few pigs, sheep and cattle. However, by the second century BC, many of these family farms had been abandoned as farmers left the countryside to join the Roman army. The old farming lands were bought by rich land owners, who created huge estates that were farmed by slaves.

By the time of the Empire, almost all farm workers were slaves. They had an exhausting life, planting and harvesting crops with very basic tools, chopping down trees to clear new fields, and looking after animals. Farms provided people in the towns with grain, olive oil, wine, meat, cheese and wool. Some Roman farms, especially in North Africa, sent their crops overseas to other parts of the Empire, and the owners of these farms became incredibly rich.

Evidence under our feet: Roman floors

WHAT DO THEY TELL US?

Although the walls of most Roman villas have long since disappeared, many of their floors have survived, buried under layers of earth. When these floors are excavated, they reveal the layout of the villa's rooms. Many surviving floors are still decorated with mosaics, which are often remarkably complete. Roman mosaics often feature geometric patterns and many show legends of the gods or scenes from country life. The floor shown here, with its striking geometric patterns, was discovered in the Roman province of Libya, northern Africa.

⋀ One of the most lavish Roman villas was built by the emperor Hadrian at Tivoli, near Rome. It was surrounded by gardens and had two bath houses, heated by the hypocaust system.

A VILLA IN THE COUNTRY

For most Roman landowners, their country villas were simply the places to which they escaped when city life became too stressful. Some villas were quite basic, but others were luxurious, with their own bathhouse and beautiful formal gardens filled with statues and ornamental pools.

Usually, the rooms of a villa were arranged around a central, enclosed garden. The rooms included a dining room, a kitchen, and a study, as well as several bedrooms for family and guests. Towards the back of the villa were store-rooms, estate offices and living quarters for the farm manager, servants, and slaves. The walls of country villas were often painted with beautiful frescoes, while their floors were laid with stunning mosaics.

Central heating: the hypocaust system

WHAT DOES IT TELL US?

Underneath the floors of some Roman villas, archaeologists have discovered evidence of an ingenious method of central heating. Known as the hypocaust system, it was powered by a fire in the basement. Hot air from the fire flowed into spaces underneath the floor and inside the villa's walls, so heating up the entire house. The hypocaust system of heating was also used in the Roman baths.

WHAT WERE ROMAN FAMILIES LIKE?

Family life was very important to the Romans. At the head of the family was the father – known as the *paterfamilias.* He led the daily family prayers and made all the big decisions for his family. However, a typical Roman father spent a lot of time away from home, leaving his wife to run the household and take care of the children's early education.

During the Roman Republic, most women had large families and stayed at home, teaching their children and spinning and weaving cloth for their families' clothes. But by the time of the Empire, many wealthy wives left all the work to their slaves. Instead, they spent their time pampering themselves and attending grand dinner parties.

ROMAN CHILDREN

Most children living in the Empire were brought up to be loyal Roman citizens. Boys from wealthy families were trained as soldiers or to work in government, and girls were prepared to be good wives.

Having fun: Roman toys

WHAT DO THEY TELL US?

Archaeologists have discovered several Roman toys, including a simple doll, some glass and pottery marbles, and some toy animals. There is also evidence that Roman children played on see-saws and swings, practised fighting with wooden swords, and even had miniature chariots that were pulled by goats or geese. The toy horse shown here could have been pushed or pulled along.

The children of traders and craft workers learned their family trade by copying their parents. Children from poor families started work as soon as they could, but richer parents sent their children to school.

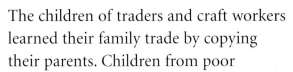

> A slave serving at a banquet, shown in a Roman mosaic.

LIFE AS A SLAVE

Many Roman families had slaves to do the hard work in their homes. Household slaves did the shopping, cooking and cleaning. They also served at meals and helped their mistress with her hair, clothes and make-up. Meanwhile, other slaves worked in shops and businesses or on farms.

Slaves were usually bought from dealers or were born into a slave family. They had no legal rights and belonged entirely to their master or mistress. But in many Roman homes, slaves were treated kindly. Some educated slaves worked as private tutors, doctors or librarians, and some were employed as government officials.

However, life was not so pleasant for other slaves. Many were forced to do hard and dangerous work in mines or on building sites. Others were trained as gladiators and had to fight to the death in the arena for public entertainment.

WHAT DID THE ROMANS WEAR?

Most Roman clothes were very simple. They were usually made from wool, which was spun and woven by hand at home or in a workshop. Sometimes, the Romans wore clothes made from Egyptian linen and some very rich people had garments made from Indian cotton or Chinese silk. Both men and women wore a lot of rings and fastened their clothes with brooches. Wealthy women also adorned themselves with gold and silver bracelets, necklaces and earrings.

MEN'S WEAR

The basic garment for men was a simple, belted tunic, that was made from two rectangles of wool stitched together. Under this tunic, a man wore a loincloth made from a strip of wool or linen. Men also wore simple cloaks, that could be wrapped around them or fastened at the neck with a brooch.

For special occasions, men and boys wore a toga over a tunic. A *toga* was a very long strip of woollen cloth, wrapped around the body and draped over one shoulder. *Togas* were usually plain white, but, until they were sixteen, boys from wealthy families wore a white *toga* with a narrow purple border. *Togas* with a broad purple border were worn by senators.

Unisex jewellery: Roman rings

WHAT DO THEY TELL US?

Many Roman rings have survived – especially in graves. These rings were worn by men as well as women. Wealthy Romans wore rings made from gold and silver set with precious stones, while rings made from bronze have been discovered in the graves of poorer people. Some Roman rings were carved from semi-precious stones, such as the amber ring shown here.

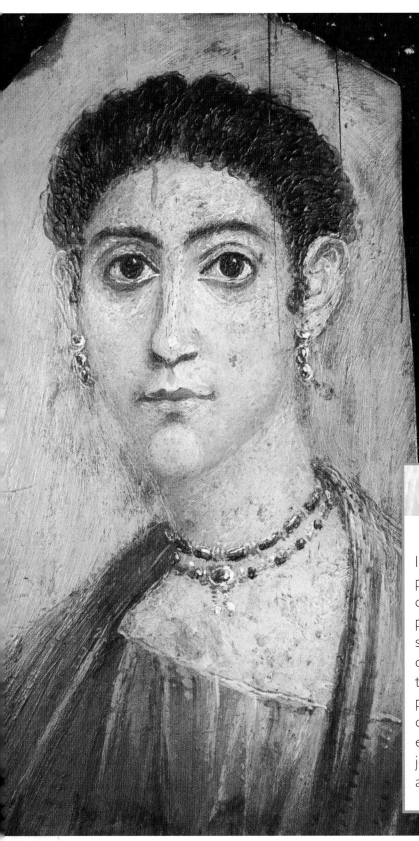

WOMEN'S WEAR

Roman women wore a long, belted sleeveless dress called a *stola*. Over this was a large rectangular shawl, known as a *palla*, which could be worn draped around the shoulders or looped over the head, like a hood. Under the *stola*, women wore a loincloth and sometimes a simple leather bra. Girls wore white until they were married, but after marriage they often wore brightly coloured dresses.

Early portraits:
coffins from Egypt

WHAT DO THEY TELL US?

In the Roman province of Egypt, people were buried in wooden coffins, with their portraits painted on the lid, like the one shown here. Several of these coffins have been discovered in the dry sands of Egypt. The coffin portraits are very lifelike and detailed. They provide valuable evidence of what Roman jewellery, hairstyles, clothing and even make-up were like.

BEAUTY CARE

Looking good was very important to the Romans, and both men and women liked to take good care of themselves. By the time of the Empire, many wealthy Roman women were spending hours every morning being made up by their slaves, and most men started the day by visiting the barber's shop for a shave.

➤ Long-handled spoons like this were used by Roman slaves to prepare cosmetics for their mistress.

Ancient make-up: Roman cosmetic equipment

WHAT DOES IT TELL US?

A range of cosmetics has survived from the time of the Roman Empire, showing the care that some Roman women lavished on their appearance. Archaeologists have found delicate glass pots and jars for holding oils, creams and perfumes. They have also discovered some slender silver spatulas which were used for mixing and applying cosmetics.

ROMAN MAKE-UP

It was very fashionable in Roman times for women to look pale, so they whitened their faces and arms with powdered chalk or a mixture made from lead that turned out to be poisonous. They darkened their eyebrows and eyelashes with soot, and painted their lips red, using plant dye or the sediment of red wine. As well as applying make-up, Roman women liked to treat their skin with a variety of preparations. They applied face-packs of bread soaked in milk and even used a cream made from crushed snails!

HAIR CARE

During the time of the Republic, most women wore their hair tied in a simple bun at the back of their head, but by the time of the Empire some very elaborate styles had developed. Wealthy women's hair was curled and braided and held in place with dozens of pins. Some women even cut off their slaves' hair and had it made into wigs or hair pieces for themselves.

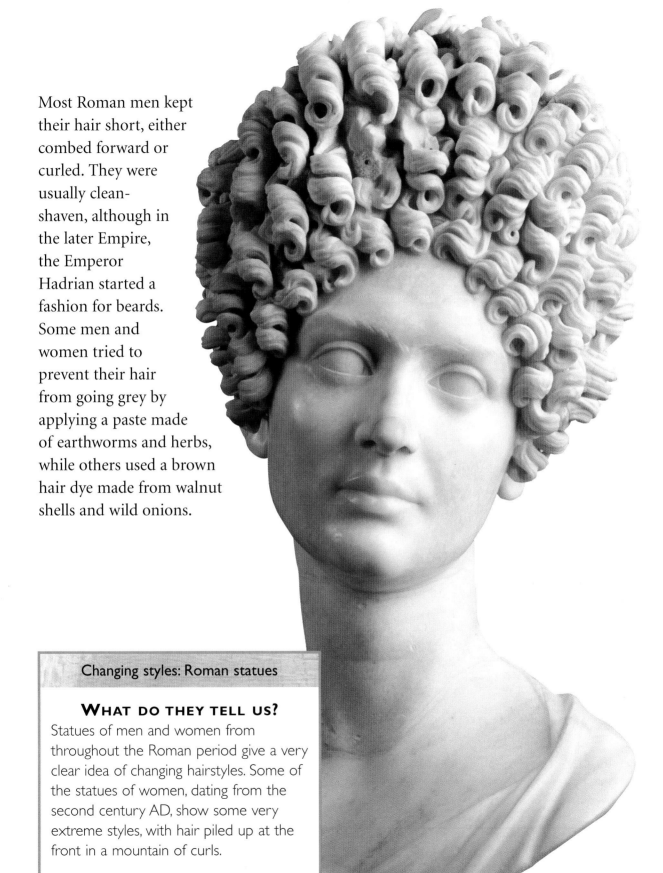

Most Roman men kept their hair short, either combed forward or curled. They were usually clean-shaven, although in the later Empire, the Emperor Hadrian started a fashion for beards. Some men and women tried to prevent their hair from going grey by applying a paste made of earthworms and herbs, while others used a brown hair dye made from walnut shells and wild onions.

Changing styles: Roman statues

WHAT DO THEY TELL US?

Statues of men and women from throughout the Roman period give a very clear idea of changing hairstyles. Some of the statues of women, dating from the second century AD, show some very extreme styles, with hair piled up at the front in a mountain of curls.

WHAT DID THE ROMANS EAT?

Many of the foods we eat today were unheard of in Roman times. The Romans had no potatoes or tomatoes, and their basic foods were probably bread, beans and lentils. Rich people had a varied diet, and cooks served up amazing dishes at banquets, but poor people's food was very plain and simple.

Poor people and slaves survived on porridge, bread and soup, but richer Romans had more interesting meals. For breakfast, they would often eat a snack of bread with honey, and lunch was usually a simple meal of eggs, cheese, cold meat and fruit. Most wealthier Romans ate very little during the day, waiting instead to eat their main meal. This usually consisted of roast poultry or fish, accompanied by lentils or beans.

Different dishes: Roman tableware

WHAT DO THEY TELL US?

A wide variety of pots and dishes have survived from Roman times, showing how Romans of all classes served up their food. Dishes range from basic polished red pots, known as Samian ware, to elaborate bowls and goblets made from silver and glass. The cup shown above is decorated with a scene from a banquet.

The Romans drank a lot of wine, which they usually flavoured with spices or sweetened with honey, and diluted with water. Poorer Romans drank water from the public fountains or from streams.

WHAT DOES IT TELL US?

When archaeologists uncovered the ruins of a large house in the buried city of Pompeii, they found the remains of a complete kitchen (shown below). This provided fascinating evidence of the way the Romans prepared and cooked their meals. The kitchen had a stone cooking stove with a set of cooking pots still standing on it. The bronze pots were heated by burning charcoal chips in a shallow tray beneath them.

LAVISH BANQUETS

Wealthy Romans had trained cooks who produced lavish banquets with many courses. Cooks competed with each other to produce exotic dishes, serving up food such as larks' tongues, mice cooked in honey, and even elephants' trunks. Rich sauces were especially popular – probably because they helped to disguise the taste of food that wasn't very fresh.

Banquets lasted for hours and included many courses, which were presented in spectacular ways. Sometimes, guests ate so much that they had to retire to a small side room, called a vomitarium, to vomit up some of their food!

Amazing amphitheatre: the Colosseum

WHAT DOES IT TELL US?

The remains of several Roman amphitheatres have been discovered in Europe and Asia, but the biggest one of all is the Colosseum in Rome, which could hold 50,000 people. It is still possible to see its tiered seats, and the small cells under the arena where prisoners and wild animals were kept.

HAVING FUN

By the time of the Empire, many people had lots of free time, because their slaves did most of the work. People flocked to watch bloody shows, known as 'the games', and also enjoyed chariot races and theatre performances.

The Roman emperors paid for spectacular public shows, which were held in vast public amphitheatres such as the Colosseum in Rome. The games featured musicians, dancers, jugglers and performing animals. Sometimes, wild beasts were released into the arena and hunted down with spears, daggers, and bows and arrows, and sometimes the arena was flooded with water and mock sea battles were fought.

Perhaps the greatest attractions of the games were the gladiator fights. Most gladiators were slaves, criminals or prisoners of war. Some female slaves were also forced to fight. The gladiators dressed in skimpy armour and fought each other in savage battles that often ended in death.

RACES AND PLAYS

Chariot races were another major crowd-puller. In a chariot race, teams of horses each pulled a chariot around a race track while the crowd cheered wildly for their favourite team. The races were incredibly wild and dangerous, and drivers and their horses were often killed.

As well as attending the games and the races, the Romans also loved to go to the theatre. Plays were usually performed in outdoor stone theatres with rows of tiered seats. At first the Romans mainly performed Latin versions of ancient

Greek comedies and tragedies, but later they invented pantomime – a more popular form of theatre. In these simple productions a chorus sang a series of songs while the actors mimed the action.

Funny faces: actors' masks

WHAT DO THEY TELL US?

Roman plays were acted by an all-male cast, and the actors wore masks to indicate the type of character they were playing. Some mosaics and carvings of actors' masks have survived, providing a good idea of what a Roman audience would have seen. The masks are simple and dramatic – intended to be seen from anywhere in the theatre. They show the typical characters that an actor might play, such as 'the virtuous maiden', 'the wise old man' or 'the smiling fool'. The mask shown above, comes from a mosaic decoration for a Roman theatre.

HOW DID THE ROMANS COMMUNICATE?

By the fifth century BC, some leading members of the Latin people knew how to read and write. The Latins learned their reading and writing skills from their northern neighbours, the Etruscans. The Latins were also strongly influenced by the Greeks, and included many Greek words in their language.

By the time the Latins founded Rome, around 750BC, they had developed a language of their own, called Latin. Gradually, this was used all over Italy. It also spread throughout the Empire, where it became the official language of government.

READING AND WRITING

Although the vast majority of people in the Roman Empire could not read or write, wealthy families all over the Empire made sure that their children had a good education. This meant learning to read and write Latin. People took pride in their ability to read, and the works of authors who wrote in Latin were widely enjoyed.

School began when a child was seven years old. Girls and boys were taught together in a primary school called a *ludus*, where they learned reading, writing and arithmetic. Pupils learned to write on re-usable wax tablets, using a pointed metal pen called a stylus.

At the age of 11 girls left school, but most boys moved on to a secondary

Pride in writing: a portrait from Pompeii

WHAT DOES IT TELL US?

This portrait found in the city of Pompeii illustrates how important writing was to the Romans. It shows a young couple who clearly wish to show the world that they are both educated. The man holds a rolled-up papyrus scroll, and may be a lawyer. The woman holds up her stylus and wax tablet, showing that she too enjoys writing.

school, known as a *grammaticus.* Here, pupils studied Greek and Roman literature, mathematics, history, geography and music. Making speeches was very important in Roman public life, so boys also studied the art of public speaking, which was known as *rhetoric.*

Ⓐ Children all over the Roman Empire were taught to read and write Latin so they could play a useful role in helping to run the provinces.

Different texts: Roman writing materials

WHAT DO THEY TELL US?

Archaeologists have found a range of writing materials, showing that the Romans used different methods for different types of writing. For unimportant texts, people either used a stylus to write on wax tablets or wrote with a pen and ink on cheap, thin slices of wood. Legal contracts were written on Egyptian papyrus (a type of paper made from reeds). The most important texts – such as works of literature – were written on vellum. Vellum was made from a thin layer of calf's skin and had a very smooth surface. By the end of the Roman period, vellum pages were sewn together to make books that were protected by leather covers.

RUNNING THE EMPIRE

Within the vast Roman Empire, people spoke many different languages, but everyone was united by the common language of Latin. All over the Empire, Latin was the language that was used by government officials, tax collectors and lawyers. This official language of government made the task of running the Empire much easier.

SENDING MESSAGES

The smooth running of the Roman Empire also depended on a very efficient transportation system and a vast network of roads covered the Empire. Roman ships made regular journeys from Italy across the Mediterranean Sea, reaching Constantinople, Northern Africa and Spain.

Built to last: Roman roads

WHAT DO THEY TELL US?

Roman roads were so well built that many of them were in daily use right up until the eighteenth century. Even today, some stretches survive showing how the Romans built their roads. First, a wide trench was dug and filled with sand. Over this a layer of gravel and stones was packed down hard. Finally, large, flat paving stones were laid over the surface of the road, and its edges were marked out with rectangular stone blocks. The road shown above is the Appian Way, which ran south through Italy from Rome.

Roman engineers designed their roads to be as direct as possible. Sometimes, when a road reached a wide, deep valley, the Romans constructed a raised road, called a viaduct, which ran right over the valley. They also built massive, arched bridges to span wide rivers.

Roman roads were even and well-paved, and the Romans made sure they were kept in good repair. This meant that messengers from all parts of the Empire could quickly carry news of any trouble to Rome. In response, a unit of soldiers could be sent to march straight to the trouble spot. Milestones were placed at regular intervals along the roads, so travellers could see how far they had to go to reach their destination.

➤ This Roman milestone still stands in Capernaum, Israel with part of its original inscription still intact.

Keeping in touch: Pliny's letters

WHAT DO THEY TELL US?

The Romans were great letter writers, and many letters survive from Roman times. The most famous Roman letter writer was Pliny the Younger, who lived from around AD61 to 113. Pliny's letters include his correspondence with the Emperor Trajan, but also many personal messages to his wife and friends. His best known letter describes the eruption of Mount Vesuvius, which destroyed the city of Pompeii and killed his uncle, Pliny the Elder.

WHO DID THE ROMANS WORSHIP?

Up until the time of the late Empire, most Romans worshipped a range of different gods. Some were grand figures, such as Apollo, the god of the sun. Others were friendly household spirits who, the Romans believed, kept watch over their homes. In the Roman provinces of the Middle East, many people followed the Jewish religion. Other people worshipped gods from Persia or Egypt, such as Mithras or Isis. However, by the fourth century AD, the most popular religion in the Roman Empire was the relatively new faith of Christianity.

MIGHTY GODS

Before the coming of Christianity, most Romans prayed to a group of powerful gods and goddesses who had first been worshipped by the Greeks. Chief amongst these gods were Jupiter, the god of the sky, and his wife Juno, the goddess of women. Each god or goddess was

Places of worship: Roman temples

WHAT DO THEY TELL US?

Several Roman temples have survived in the city of Rome and the Roman provinces. These impressive buildings show how a public temple was laid out. At the front of the temple was a flight of steps, leading to a covered area. This was where the priests offered sacrifices to the god to whom the temple was dedicated. At the back was a private room. This was the sacred part of the temple where the statue of the god was kept. Only priests were allowed in this area. The temple shown here was dedicated to Portumnus, the god of harbours and ports. It was built on the banks of the River Tiber in Rome around the year 100BC.

WHAT DO THEY TELL US?

During the first century AD, the Roman poet Ovid wrote a series of poems based on the legends of the gods. One of the most famous of these poems tells how the goddess Juno turned Ariadne the weaver into a spider, as a punishment for daring to love the great god Jupiter. Ovid's poems were widely read in Roman times, and they reveal the richness of the Roman legends.

responsible for a different area of life. The Romans prayed to Mars (the god of war) for victory in battle and asked Venus to grant them success in love.

➢ The chief Roman god was Jupiter, who was also the god of thunder and lightning. When he was angry the Romans believed he hurled thunderbolts from the sky.

As well as saying prayers, the Romans sacrificed animals to the gods. Priests slaughtered oxen, sheep, pigs and doves on open-air altars in front of temples. After a creature was killed, its internal organs were taken out and examined. The Romans believed that the pattern made by the organs helped them discover the will of the gods.

ROMAN PRIESTS

Many Roman priests had other jobs as well, and the chief priest was the emperor himself. However, one group of priestesses, known as the vestal virgins, devoted most of their lives to serving their goddess. The vestal virgins were chosen at the age of seven and spent the next 30 years living in the temple of Vesta in Rome. Vesta was the goddess of the earth and it was the vestal virgins' sacred duty to keep a fire burning constantly in her temple. The Romans believed that disaster would strike the state if this fire was ever allowed to go out.

GOD OF HEALING

One of the Romans' favourite gods was Aesculapias, the god of healing. Medicine was not very advanced in Roman times, so people often asked the gods to cure them of their diseases. Some people were so desperate for cures that they spent all night in the temple of Aesculapias in Rome.

Asking for help: votive offerings

WHAT DO THEY TELL US?

Many small gifts, known as votive offerings, have been discovered in Roman temples dedicated to the god of healing. These offerings take the form of metal plaques or stone carvings showing ears, legs and eyes, as shown here. Experts believe that these gifts were given either as thanks for a cure, or as reminders of a request for healing.

WHAT DOES IT TELL US?

Archaeologists have discovered several household shrines inside Roman homes. One of these shrines was found in a house at Pompeii. It consists of a simple niche in the wall with a small, stone altar. On the altar stood a group of statuettes, representing the household gods, while a pot found in front of the altar may have originally contained an offering to these gods.

HOUSEHOLD GODS

Not all worship in Roman times was carried out by priests in temples. In their own homes, the Romans worshipped two kinds of gods, who were belived to look after their household. The *lares* were spirits who protected the home, while the *penates* looked after the larder and the food stores.

Each Roman house had its own shrine where the family held daily prayers. It was called the *lararium* and it contained small statues of the *lares* and *penates*. Here, Roman families offered food, wine and flowers to their household gods. On special occasions, such as birthdays and weddings, the *lares* and *penates* were given extra gifts.

GODS FROM THE EAST

By the first century AD, many Romans were losing respect for the old gods and goddesses. Instead, they began to turn to the religions of the East. These foreign faiths had strict rules on how people should live. They also offered their followers the promise of personal salvation and life in heaven after their death.

ISIS AND MITHRAS

Two of the most popular gods from the East were Isis, from Egypt, and Mithras, from Persia. Thousands of Roman women became passionate followers of Isis after the Egyptian Queen Cleopatra spent a year in Rome in 45BC. The Persian god Mithras was especially popular with Roman soldiers. Followers of Mithras gathered in underground temples, where they suffered terrifying tests, such as being locked in a coffin for hours.

Religious rattle: a priest's sistrum

WHAT DOES IT TELL US?

Several metal rattles have been found in ruined Roman temples devoted to the Egyptian goddess Isis. Carvings, like the one shown here, of ceremonies indicate that priests shook a rattle (known as a sistrum) during their services. The rattles produced a delicate clinking sound.

JEWS AND CHRISTIANS

In the area of the Empire that is now the Middle East, many people followed the ancient religion of Judaism. Then, around 30AD, the new religion of Christianity began to spread from Jerusalem. Both Jews and Christians believe that there is only one God, which meant they couldn't worship Roman gods as well. This led the Roman emperors to conduct fierce campaigns against the Jews and Christians. Emperor Hadrian tried to stamp out Judaism completely. Nero sent hundreds of Christians to the arena to be torn apart by wild beasts, and Emperor Diocletian had thousands of people executed for refusing to give up their Christian faith.

THE RISE OF CHRISTIANITY

In AD312 Emperor Constantine finally allowed Christians to worship freely, and in AD391 Christianity was declared the official religion of the Roman Empire. By the end of the fourth century, Christian monasteries and churches were being built throughout the Empire.

Underground worship: Christian catacombs

WHAT DO THEY TELL US?

Archaeologists working in the city of Rome have discovered a series of underground chapels, in which early Christians met to worship in secret. Known as the catacombs, they were originally used as burial chambers. Some of the catacombs still have stone altars and the remains of Bible scenes painted on their walls. They provide a vivid impression of the way the early Christians worshipped.

WHAT DID THE ROMANS CONTRIBUTE TO THE WORLD?

ʌ The 19th century illustration above shows flowers with their Latin names beside them.

The Romans had an enormous impact on the world. Even though the Roman Empire came to an end over 1500 years ago, people still use Latin words every day. Architects design buildings in the Roman style, and modern city life owes a great deal to the Romans. Lawyers and politicians today still follow some ancient Roman practices, and some Christmas and many modern wedding celebrations are based on Roman festivals.

USING LATIN

After the Roman Empire collapsed in AD476, the Roman Catholic Church kept the Latin language alive. Church services were held in Latin and monks copied out a range of Roman texts. For hundreds of years, people have studied authors who wrote in Latin and some children today still learn Latin in school. Scientists give Latin names to animals and plants. This use of a common scientific language means that the same names can be used all over the world.

LATIN ROOTS

By the time the Roman Empire came to an end, Latin was the official language all over the Empire. All the languages spoken in the Empire were influenced by Latin. Italian, French and Spanish all come directly from Latin. Even the English language, which is not so closely related to Latin, still includes hundreds of words with Latin roots. For example, our word 'school' comes from the Latin word *schola*. We also use Latin phrases in our daily speech – such as *et cetera*, which means 'and the rest'.

ROMAN LETTERS AND MONTHS

Of the 26 letters in our alphabet, 22 come from the Roman alphabet. The Romans had no W or Y. V was used for U and V, and the letters I and J were both written as I.

Most of our months have Roman names. March is named after Mars, the god of war, and June gets its name from the goddess Juno. In the Roman calendar, September, October, November and December were originally the seventh, eighth, ninth and tenth months of the year. The months of July and August were named after Julius Caesar and the Emperor Augustus. All these names suggest that our calendar is based on a Roman system for calculating dates.

LAWYERS AND SENATORS

In most Roman courts, cases were tried by a judge and a jury, and this type of trial has been copied all over the world. Roman lawyers also wrote down a vast set of laws, and these have provided the models for many modern laws.

As well as copying Roman laws, people have been influenced by the Roman method of government – especially that of the Roman Republic. After the American Revolution, many Americans saw the Roman Republic as a shining example of a state without a king. They set up a republic with a senate and senators, and based their senate on the Roman senate at the time of the Republic.

BUILDING LIKE THE ROMANS

After the Empire collapsed, many cities fell into ruins and the secrets of the Roman builders were almost forgotten. However, by the fifteenth century architects in Italy became very interested in Roman architecture. They copied the Romans and constructed grand public buildings with massive columns and rounded arches. This impressive style

---

Amazing aqueduct: the Pont du Gard

WHAT DOES IT TELL US?

The Pont du Gard in southern France is part of an elaborate Roman water system (or aqueduct) that carried water from the mountains to the city of Nimes. It consists of three layers of arches, built one above the other, with a channel for water running along the top. The Pont du Gard has survived for over two thousand years, and provides a stunning example of the skill of the Roman engineers. Centuries later, modern city planners still copy the methods used by the Roman aqueduct builders.

△ Ever since the 15th century, people have built grand structures in the Roman style. The Arc de Triomphe in Paris is modelled on a Roman victory arch.

proved very popular, and soon spread throughout Europe.

ANCIENT CELEBRATIONS

Many of our present-day celebrations have their origins in ancient Rome. For example, the way we celebrate Christmas today is partly based on the Roman feast of Saturnalia. At this midwinter feast, people cooked huge meals, played games and exchanged gifts. Today's wedding customs are also strongly influenced by the Romans. When a Roman couple got engaged, the girl was given a ring to wear on the third finger of her left hand. On her wedding day, the bride wore a white dress and a garland of flowers in her hair.

LIVING LIKE THE ROMANS

Many of our towns and cities follow the Roman pattern, with grand public buildings in the centre, and streets laid out in a regular grid. Our roads, sewage and water systems are similar to those built by the Romans. People live in houses with central heating, eat food in snack bars, and visit public swimming pools and vast sports arenas – just as the Romans did two thousand years ago.

TIMELINE

BC

c.750 The Latin people found the city of Rome

c.500 Rome becomes a Republic

c.200 The Romans begin to conquer lands beyond Italy

146 The Romans control Greece

133 The Romans control large areas of the Middle East

51 The Romans conquer Gaul (present-day France)

49 Julius Caesar seizes power in Rome

44 Julius Caesar is assassinated

30 The Romans conquer Egypt

27 Augustus becomes the first Roman emperor

AD

c.30 Jesus Christ is crucified and the Christian religion begins

43 The Romans conquer Britain

117 Trajan wins land in Eastern Europe. The Roman Empire reaches its largest size.

c.200 Barbarian tribes start to launch attacks on the Roman Empire

312 Constantine allows Christians to worship in the Empire

330 Constantine moves the Empire's capital to Constantinople

394 Christianity becomes the official religion of the Roman Empire

395 The Roman Empire splits permanently in two

476 Rome is invaded by Visigoths. The Roman Empire in the west collapses

1453 The Roman Empire in the east is defeated by a Turkish army

FIND OUT MORE

Fiona Chandler, Sam Taplin, Jane Bingham, *The Usborne Encyclopedia of the Roman World* (Usborne, 2001)

Terry Deary, *Rotten Romans (Horrible Histories)* (Scholastic, 1997)

Simon James, *Ancient Rome* (Eyewitness Guides) (Dorling Kindersley, 1990)

Andrew Solway, Stephen Biesty, *Rome* (Oxford University Press, 2003)

Andrew Solway, Peter Connoly, *Ancient Rome* (Oxford University Press, 2001)

HELPFUL WEBSITES

http://www.pbs.org/empires/romans/
A website produced by the American Public Broadcasting Service. The site is divided into four sections for The Roman World, Ancient Voices, the Social Order and Life in Roman Times. It also has a detailed timeline.

http://www.bbc.co.uk/schools/romans/
A BBC site designed especially for schools. Includes activities and suggestions for 'More to explore'.

http://www.roman-empire.net/
An extremely detailed site, including sections on Roman place names, pictures from Rome and photographs of battle re-enactments.

http://www.crystalinks.com/romearchitecture.html
Stunning photographs of Ancient Roman sites

http://www.romans-in-britain.org.uk/
A detailed site on the Romans in Britian. Includes a list of Roman sites in Britain and biographies of key figures.

GLOSSARY

amphitheatre   a large, stone, circular building with many seats, where people went to watch gladiator fights

arena   the central area or stage of an amphitheatre

breast plate   a plate made from metal or leather, which was strapped onto a soldier's chest to protect him

cavalry   soldiers who ride horses

centurion   an officer in the Roman army who led a group of soldiers called a *century*

chariot   a vehicle with four wheels, pulled by horses, which was sometimes used for races

colony   land that is controlled by rulers from a foreign country. The Romans had many colonies, which were all ruled from Rome

conquer   to overcome an enemy and win land

consul   During the Roman Republic, the consuls were the leaders of the government (senate)

council   a group of important people, who meet together to make plans about how to run their country

empire   all the lands that were controlled by the Romans. The term 'Roman Empire' also refers to the period from 27BC to AD476, when Rome was ruled by emperors

fresco   a picture painted on a wall while the plaster is still damp

gladiator   someone who was trained to fight in the arena to entertain the Roman people. Gladiators were often slaves

governor   someone who ran a province (or region) in the Roman Empire

legion   someone who served in the roman army. Legionaires were usually foot solders

loincloth   a piece of cloth used to cover the waist and hips

mosaic   a picture made up of hundreds of small pieces of stone, marble or glass

philosopher   someone who thinks very carefully about human life and how it should be lived

province   a region of the Roman Empire outside Italy that was ruled by a governor

republic   a country without a king or a queen, whose rulers are elected by the people. The Roman Republic lasted from 510BC to 27BC

senate   the group of men who governed Rome during the Roman Republic

senator   a member of the senate.

stylus   a thin metal rod, used like a pen to write on wax tablets

toga   a long piece of cloth worn draped around their body by Roman men

tribe   a group of people who share the same descendants, laws and customs

villa   a large and comfortable Roman house in the country

votive offering   a gift offered to the gods, in the hope that the gods will help the giver in some way

INDEX

actors 31

Aesculapias 38

amphitheatres 30, 31

Appian Way 34

aqueducts 44

architecture 5, 44-5

army 6, 10, 11, 12-15

Augustus, Emperor 5, 11, 43

banquets 16, 28, 29

baths 6, 18-19, 21

Britain 5, 13, 14, 15

Byzantine Empire 7

Caesar, Julius 10, 11, 13, 14, 43

Caligula, Emperor 11

Caracalla, Emperor 19

catacombs 41

chariot races 4, 30, 31

children 22, 23

clothes 18, 22, 24-5

Colosseum, Rome 30, 31

Commodus, Emperor 11

Constantine, Emperor 11, 41

death 18, 40

Diocletian, Emperor 41

education 22, 32-3

Empire, Roman 5, 6, 7, 11, 12, 15, 34

Etruscans 4, 8, 32

everyday life 16-31

family life 22-3

farming 20

food 17, 28-9

forts 12, 15

games 30-1

gladiator fights 4, 11, 23, 31

gods/goddesses 6, 36-40

Greeks 4-5, 31, 32, 33, 36, 40

Hadrian, Emperor 15, 21, 41

Hadrian's Wall 15

hairstyles 26-7

household gods 39

houses 16-17, 39

jewellery 17, 18, 24, 25

Latin (language) 31, 32, 33, 34, 42

Latins 4, 31, 32

law and order 6, 34, 42, 44

Livy 8

make-up 26

Marcus Aurelius, Emperor 11

Mithras 36, 40

mosaics 17, 20, 21, 23, 31

Nero, Emperor 11, 41

numbers/numerals 4

Ovid 37

plays 31

plebeians 9

Pliny the Younger 35

Plutarch 10

Pompeii 16, 17, 29, 32, 35, 39

priests 36, 37, 38, 39, 40

religion 5, 36-41

Republic, Roman 9, 10, 11, 22, 44

roads 12, 34-5

Rome 4, 6, 7, 8, 9, 10, 19, 30, 36, 41

schools 23, 32-3

Senate/senators 9, 10, 44

shops 6, 16, 17

shrines 39

slaves 20, 21, 23

soldiers 12-14, 22, 35

Suetonius 11

Tarquinus Superbus 8, 9

taxation 6, 34

temples 4, 6, 36, 37, 38, 39

theatres 6, 30, 31

Tiber, River 4, 36

Tiberius, Emperor 11

Titus, Emperor 11

towns 6, 16-17, 45

toys 22

trade 7

Trajan, Emperor 11, 13, 35

Trajan's Column 13

vestal virgins 38

villas 16, 20, 21

weapons 13, 14